Original title:
Tying the Ties

Copyright © 2025 Creative Arts Management OÜ
All rights reserved.

Author: Victor Mercer
ISBN HARDBACK: 978-1-80586-133-1
ISBN PAPERBACK: 978-1-80586-605-3

Interwoven Lives

In a world of tangled threads,
We weave our laughs and grins.
Each twist a tale, a joyride,
We stumble, trip, then spin.

A sock lost in the laundry heap,
Becomes a saga of our play.
With every knot, a story deep,
We dance through night and day.

The Unity of Threads

A shoelace fights, a ribbon strains,
Yet still they hold on tight.
Through ups and downs and silly games,
They find a way to light.

In mismatched colors, patterns bright,
They laugh at fate's design.
Their unity in chaos, right,
A tangled heart divine.

The Lifeline of Relationships

Friendship's cords stretch far and wide,
Sometimes they break and fray.
But with a wink and goofy slide,
We knot them back to play.

Like shoelaces tied in bows so grand,
We skip along the way.
No matter how we try and plan,
The humor's here to stay.

Knots of Shared Dreams

We tie our dreams in curious knots,
With laughter as the glue.
A bundle of hopes in silly spots,
We seek the bright and new.

With every twist, we make it fun,
A friendship full of cheer.
Our shared missteps weigh a ton,
Yet still, we persevere.

A Cloak of Companionship

In a world of threads and fray,
Laughter stitches night and day.
With every knot, we dance around,
In this cozy chaos, joy is found.

Worn cheeky hats, mismatched shoes,
Our colorful quirks, none to lose.
Together we stumble, trip, and tease,
A perfect patchwork, life's a breeze.

The Symphony of Seams

Listen close, the fabric sings,
A whimsical tune that laughter brings.
Each seam a note, each button a beat,
In this wacky dance, we can't be beat.

With threads of humor intertwined,
We laugh at tangles, never maligned.
A symphony of silly, a melody bright,
In stitches and giggles, we take flight.

Embracing Interdependence

With arms around in playful fashion,
We trip through life with joyous passion.
A tug here, a pull there, we mangle and mix,
Our laughter erupts in these curious tricks.

In the tapestry of friendship's embrace,
We find our strength, we find our place.
With every twist and little tug,
We spin merry tales, dance in a hug.

Entwined Destinies

Two shoelaces in a knot so tight,
We roam the world, a curious sight.
Side by side, we wander and sway,
In our silly bond, come what may.

Like mismatched socks on a Sunday morn,
We chase the whims, both ragged and worn.
In tangled adventures, we find our way,
With giggles that brighten the cloudiest day.

Embracing the Tangle

In knots of joy we find our way,
A shoelace here, a squirrel there.
Giggling at the fray of day,
As pants snag on chairs without a care.

We twist and turn, a wild dance,
A ribbon caught on a passing breeze.
With every mishap, we take a chance,
To laugh at life with playful ease.

The Fabric of Memories

Unraveled threads from days gone by,
A patchwork quilt of silly schemes.
Laughter stitched with a wink and sigh,
Moments sewn into our dreams.

Grandma's apron, a tale in fold,
Spills and thrills of pudding fights.
In these fibers, our love unfolds,
Knotting shadows into bright lights.

Connected Journeys

Two squirrels chase a runaway tail,
In the park amidst giggles galore.
Every twist and turn a comical trail,
Bounding forward to discover more.

Friends tied in silly shenanigans,
With a jump rope and an old dog's bark.
Every trip spawns wild plans,
Creating mischief from dawn till dark.

Interlaced Hopes

In tangled vines of dreams we blunder,
Chasing wishes that pop and sway.
A lively mess, a joyful thunder,
As we wrap our hopes in a quirky way.

With every twist, our laughter beams,
Like spaghetti caught in a funny fling.
Together we weave our silly schemes,
A silly song that all of us sing.

Crossed Threads of Fate

In a world where socks go astray,
Two mismatched pairs decide to play.
They dance around the laundry room,
Spreading oddities as they zoom!

With threads entwined from here to there,
They weave a tale beyond compare.
A yarn of laughter, bright and bold,
In every knot, a secret told.

The Net of Community

In the town where folks collect,
A web of friendships, quite direct.
With cookies shared and shoes exchanged,
It's never dull, just a bit deranged!

We pitch our tents in the schoolyard sun,
Each tangle making life more fun.
With every laugh and every cheer,
We catch the joy, and hold it near.

Woven Whispers

In a cafe where chatter flows,
A table's full of highs and lows.
With stories woven, tales collide,
Like threads that twist, they can't divide.

A tale of mishaps, spills and laughs,
With every sip, we share our gaffes.
The fabric of our lives so bright,
Stitched together, what a sight!

Ties that Weathered Storms

Through rainy days and messy nights,
We gather close, sharing our sights.
With umbrellas flipped and laughter shared,
We're knit together, none are scared.

When winds blow hard and slingshots fly,
Our spirits lift, we can't deny.
In every storm, we find the grace,
Of bonds that time cannot erase.

The Circle of Connection

Round and round, we dance with glee,
With every twist, a laugh from me.
Like a game of tug, we pull and play,
In this circle, we find our way.

Laughter echoes, we trip and stumble,
On this merry ride, we giggle and grumble.
Holding on tight, we give it a spin,
In the circle, that's where we grin.

Tethered Souls

We're like two balloons, tied with a string,
Floating together, oh what joy we bring!
You float up high, while I hug the ground,
Together we laugh, our joy knows no bound.

Sometimes I tangle, as you take a dive,
One twist too many, oh we just survive!
But in this mess, we find pure delight,
Tethered, we shine, like stars in the night.

The Knots of Connection

We tie the knots, oh what a maze,
Filling our days with silly ways.
One day a bow, the next a mess,
Each twist and turn, brings more than jest.

Like shoelaces flopping, we trip and fall,
But laughter rings loud, it conquers all.
In this tangled dance, we sway to the beat,
Knots of connection, oh, life is sweet!

Weaving Bonds of Heart

With strings of laughter, we weave our tale,
Creating a bond that will never frail.
Every stitch a joke, a tickle, a grin,
In this fabric of friendship, we're bound to win.

So grab a thread, let's tie up a laugh,
We'll stitch together our fun-filled craft.
In the quilt of our days, we're never apart,
Just weaving and laughing, is the work of the heart.

Embracing the Unknown

To join your socks with mine, oh dear,
A fashion statement, loud and clear.
With mismatched prints, we bravely stroll,
In a world where odd is the new goal.

Coffee stains on our favorite shirt,
Who knew fashion could be such a quirt?
We laugh it off with a jovial cheer,
Embrace the chaos, let's make it clear.

Curved Pathways

We walk in loops, a spiral dance,
Cotton strings in a playful prance.
Twisted ankle, but what a sight,
We giggle through this comic plight.

Your shoelaces tie me in a knot,
Navigating life with a goofy plot.
Every corner, bumps, and slides,
Together we roll, with luck as our guides.

The Unbreakable Loop

In silly hats, we make our stand,
With silly clips held in our hand.
The clumsy moves, a flailing grace,
Life's a circus, let's embrace the space.

A jammed-up car, we can't get through,
But we'll make a smile, just me and you.
Through tangled cords, we find delight,
In the dance of knots, our spirits ignite.

Ties That Bind

Every friendship has its quirks,
With rubber bands and funly jerks.
We pull, we stretch, but never break,
In laughter's grip, we both partake.

A pizza party, a noodle war,
We laugh and tie up a pasta score.
With sauce on hands, who needs a plate?
In this wild ride, let's celebrate!

The Fabric of Feelings

In a patchwork world, we dance and spin,
With mismatched socks, we laugh and grin.
Threading our joys like silly string,
Heartfelt giggles, that's our thing.

A button pops, a seam unravels,
We chase each other through fabric travels.
With every stitch, we mend the tear,
Creating moments, we joyfully share.

A Tapestry of Togetherness

We weave our tales with yarns so bright,
Silly patterns that bring delight.
Knots of laughter, spun with glee,
This tangled mess is family.

Frayed edges whisper tales of old,
Threads of friendship, purest gold.
In this quilt of fun, we find a place,
A colorful patchwork, full of grace.

Binds of Belonging

With silly string and crazy glue,
We stick together, just me and you.
A clumsy hug, a tug, a pull,
In this crazy mix, our hearts are full.

Together we float on balloons of air,
Making memories beyond compare.
In a world of chaos, we stand aligned,
With bonds so strong, our hearts entwined.

The Stitch of Kindred Spirits

Like needles pricking, we find our way,
Through wobbly paths, we crave to play.
An awkward dance, the rhythm's wrong,
But in our hearts, we sing along.

Threads of humor, a patchwork cheer,
Embroidered smiles, we hold so dear.
In this goofy quilt of love and fun,
Together forever, we'll never be done.

The Chain of Moments

In every knot, a laugh we find,
A silly twist, a memory blind.
Through thick and thin, we weave our fates,
With tangled yarns and outlandish mates.

A loop of joy, a playful chain,
Where jokes are shared, and fun is plain.
We trip and stumble, but what a show,
In this wild ride, we steal the glow.

Each bend and twist, a tale to tell,
Of awkward hugs and slip-ups swell.
In laughter stitched, our bond is tight,
A colorful mess, what pure delight!

So here we are, in this grand spree,
With giggles vibrant, oh let it be!
In every moment, a thread we weave,
Creating chaos, yet we believe!

Holding Tight Our Stories

With a silly grip, our tales unfold,
We clutch them close, though they're oft' retold.
In a whirl of quirks, they dance and spin,
Each twist a giggle, where fun begins.

From clumsy blunders to winking eyes,
We hold our dreams, but oh, what a prize!
In won't-let-go moments, we find our cheer,
As laughter echoing pulls us near.

With frayed edges and tales absurd,
We tie them tight, though truth gets blurred.
In this raucous hold, we find delight,
Sharing our stories till late at night.

So come join us in this tangled game,
Where punchlines hit and no one's the same.
In every hug, we're weaving fate,
A funny chronicle, can't wait, can't wait!

A Dance of Ties

Two left feet on this dance floor,
We spin and tangle, but want some more!
A whirl of fabrics, all colors bright,
Each step a snafu, but what a sight!

With laughter shared and partners lost,
We shimmy and shake, never counting the cost.
In every trip, a chuckle breaks free,
Who knew this dance could bring such glee?

With spins and flips, we find our place,
Each falter a gem in this silly space.
We twine together, a giggly crew,
In the most ridiculous steps we do!

As we flop and fall, we feel the ties,
In messy moments, a joy that flies.
So with a wink and a hearty cheer,
Let's dance away, with no end near!

The Strength in Weaving

With laughter strong, we pull the thread,
In this crazy quilt, no need for dread.
Pieces stitched with joy and glee,
A patchwork of quirks, just you and me.

From silly memes to goofy faces,
We craft our bonds through wild embraces.
In every poke and playful tease,
We weave a friendship that aims to please.

Frayed at times, but oh, so bright,
A colorful cloth, a beloved sight.
In every fold, a story hides,
Of wild adventures and fun-filled rides.

So let's grab some thread and make it fun,
In this tapestry, we are all one.
For in the strength of our woven tale,
We find the love that will never fail!

The Seam of Togetherness

In a world of knots we dwell,
Threads of laughter, stories to tell.
Sewing moments, side by side,
With stitches of joy, we take our ride.

Laughing as the fabric frays,
Each slip up, a new ballet.
With every twist, a tale unfolds,
In this tapestry, our hearts are bold.

Our mismatched patterns, a sight to see,
Together we make the best of debris.
Through the seams, we patch the fun,
Stitching memories, one by one.

So let us dance in the tangled yarn,
Creating chaos, but no need to fawn.
For in our mess, a beauty shines,
In this delightful thread of lines.

Bound by Destiny

Two left feet on the dance floor,
Tripping over fate, we ask for more.
Destined to laugh at our missteps,
These funny ties, our hearts accepts.

We stumble here, we fumble there,
Bound together in awkward flair.
With every twist and silly turn,
We learn to laugh and brightly burn.

The universe giggles at our plight,
Sending us bumps to ignite the light.
With every tether that seems intent,
We find the joy, the laughter's scent.

So here's to bonds that make us grin,
In this crazy game, we always win.
Tangled yet free, we waltz along,
With our jumbled ties, we'll sing our song.

Knotted Hearts

With a heart that's often skewed,
We tie ourselves in laughter brewed.
Each knot a giggle, unforeseen,
As we dance like fools, so keen.

Love's a rope that sometimes slips,
Tied up together, with silly quips.
Like shoelaces loose, always in play,
Our knotted hearts lead the way.

JB and I are a comical pair,
Bound by humor, floating in air.
Every twist is a cause for cheer,
In our entangled lives, there's nothing to fear.

So let us knot and laugh out loud,
In the fabric of life, we're feeling proud.
With every tug, our bond grows tight,
In the threads of joy, we take our flight.

The Connection We Weave

Gather round, let's spin a yarn,
Weaving tales, like a farmer's barn.
Every stitch, a quirky jest,
In this tapestry, we find our nest.

With needle and thread, we play a game,
Each strand a laugh, never the same.
We connect the dots in fits of glee,
As we weave our stories, wild and free.

Twists and turns in our crazy loom,
Breaking rules as we make room.
Tape measure's lost, but who needs that?
As we bind our laughs, what's the format?

So here's to the ties, grotesque and grand,
In this patchwork quilt, hand in hand.
Through the giggles, the knots we see,
Making connections, endlessly.

Threads of Togetherness

In a room full of laughter, we weave our fate,
The yarn of our moments, oh isn't it great?
With knots made of giggles and loops of delight,
We stitch our adventures from morning to night.

A sock and a shoe, they dance on the floor,
One snags on the other, they tumble and roar.
Like threads tangled up in a bowl of spaghetti,
Each twist tells a story, each turn is confetti.

Our stories entwined, like a cat with a ball,
We roll through the chaos, we stumble and sprawl.
Each bump in the road is a yarn to be spun,
With laughter and love, oh, we're never outdone!

So let's gather our threads, let the colors collide,
In this crazy patchwork, we're side by side.
With a tug and a pull, we create the art,
These threads of togetherness bind every heart.

Interlaced Journeys

Two squirrels on a branch, sharing their nuts,
With acorns a-plenty, and plans that are guts!
They leap and they bound, in bewildering haps,
Each tumble, a giggle, oh, how time zaps!

Two maps rolled together, exploring the land,
One's going in circles, the other can't stand.
With a fold and a crease, they get all entwined,
Finding their way home, oh, how they've aligned!

Our puddles are splashed with umbrellas in tow,
Who knew that a storm would create quite the show?
With ducks in a row, we laugh through the splash,
Like fabric that's stitched, oh the fun we'll amass!

On journeys unpredictable, we skip and we twirl,
Each bend in the road makes our heads want to whirl.
With friendships interlaced, and mischief in sight,
We grab life's reins tightly; let's laugh 'til twilight!

The Embrace of Friendship

A bear and a rabbit, with hugs full of glee,
They roll down the hill, what a sight to see!
With laughter that echoes, we're caught in the rush,
Together we tumble, both bright as a blush.

Two pancakes, stacked high, they're ready to flip,
The syrup is funny, watch it drip off the tip!
With each syrupy layer, our jokes pile up high,
In this scrumptious embrace, let the laughter fly!

A key and a lock, such a curious pair,
Together they giggle, with secrets to share.
Although one's getting rusty and one's feeling proud,
Together they chuckle, no need for a crowd.

In this embrace of friendship, let's dance through the night,
With quirks and odd tales, oh, what pure delight!
As we hug, we discover, we're just like popcorn,
Popping with joy, in a friendship reborn!

Bound by Affection

A cactus and flower, side by side grow,
One's spiky and prickly, the other's a show.
Yet together they laugh, in the warm desert sun,
With hugs a bit tricky, but it's all in good fun!

A sandwich and pickle, quite the odd pair,
They sit in a lunchbox, with giggles to share.
As the bread holds it all, like glue on the plate,
Their bond, oh so tasty, who knew it was fate?

A spoon meets a fork, what a curious dance,
In a bowl full of noodles, they twirl and prance.
With noodle-slinging antics, they mix up the vibe,
This kitchen's a circus – geometry tribe!

Bound by affection, like socks on a line,
We tumble and trip, oh, how we so shine!
Through ups and downs, we stick like a glue,
With humor and joy, it's a colorful view!

Ribbons of Resonance

In a world of knots and bows,
Strings are tangled, but who knows?
Laughing at the silly sights,
We often trip on our own heights.

Colors flying everywhere,
A purple bow, a polka-dot scare.
We dance around with frisky flair,
In this chaos, we all share.

When crisscrossed arms take their stance,
Avoiding fate's accidental dance.
A ribbon here, a shoelace there,
All pulling us into a square!

So let us skip and let us loop,
As laughter forms the silliest group.
Together we find our entangled fun,
In this join-up race, we are all one.

Fastened by Fate

A button here, a string pulled tight,
A wardrobe duel in the morning light.
Socks that vanish, shirts that clash,
In this wild game, we all must dash.

Fashion's fickle; what a tease!
Fate's the tailor, if you please.
We wear mismatched pieces with delight,
And claim it's art with all our might!

Twirling with buttons that just won't stay,
Endless laughter's the price we pay.
For every stitch that ends in glee,
We wear our quirks like a badge, you see?

With every laugh, the seams may burst,
Yet we find joy in the zany first.
Together we zip, buckle, and tie,
As humor threads through the silly sky.

Unity in Twist and Turn

Spin in circles, with a wink,
Married laces in a blink.
Twisting tales that bind us tight,
Our jumbled steps make it all right.

Here's a flip, there goes a bend,
Each jump brings us closer, friend.
In the mix, it's pure delight,
We're all just knotted up tonight!

A twirl that leads us off the chart,
In every twist, we find the heart.
We share our giggles, unaware,
That chaos brings the best compare.

Hands together, we take the chance,
To humor selves in this silly dance.
No fancy rules, no map to find,
Just joyous joys all intertwined.

Stitched Stories

Each yarn we weave into the night,
A patchwork quilt of pure delight.
Mismatched bits with tales to tell,
In every seam, there rings a bell.

We stitch our laughter, thread by thread,
A tale of socks that always spread.
With needles raised and hearts that soar,
In this crazy craft, we want more!

Some threads unravel, some bows may break,
Yet in this fabric, friendships wake.
Lost in stitches, happy and free,
Our quirks become a wild spree.

So gather 'round and share your thread,
In this tapestry of joy, we're fed.
For every stitch and every grin,
We spin our stories — let the fun begin!

Woven in Time

From socks that lost their match,
To shirts that tried to dance,
We stitch our funny stories,
In a patchwork of romance.

The tangled yarn of laughter,
Wraps us in a giddy spree,
Each knot a giggled secret,
As silly as can be!

With every twist and braid,
Life's fabric starts to fray,
But every thread we gather,
Turns dull to bright and gay.

So let's all grab our needles,
And poke at life with glee,
For in this woven wonder,
We find our jubilee!

Patched with Memories

A jacket torn in places,
Each patch a tale to tell,
Of fun times and odd moments,
Where we all fell and fell.

The buttons so mismatched,
Like friends from different lands,
But when we're sewn together,
We bounce like rubber bands.

We'll quilt our silly snickering,
With threads of brightest hue,
Wrap our hearts in joy's fabric,
And wear our laughter too!

Every rip is just a chapter,
In this book of chuckles bright,
We mend the seams of moments,
With stitches made of light.

The Bond of Trust

Two shoelaces intertwined,
In steps both big and small,
They tangle up in mischief,
Always ready for a sprawl.

A friendship like a bowline,
Secure, yet free to roam,
Laughing at the trip-ups,
While making chaos home.

Together they find rhythm,
In every floppy flop,
When one begins to wobble,
The other helps them stop.

So if you trip in laughter,
Or stumble in your stride,
Just look for that companion,
Who'll always walk beside!

Seams of Support

A patchwork quilt of kindness,
Sewn up with care and cheer,
When life unravels softly,
It's friends who draw us near.

With needles dipped in humor,
We stitch the tales we weave,
Each poke a gentle nudge,
In the fabric of believe.

The seams may stretch and tremble,
But laughter holds us tight,
In the wobbles of our journeys,
We find our shared delight.

So let's gather all our patches,
And celebrate the ride,
For in these seams of laughter,
Together we abide!

Bonds Beyond the Horizon

In a world of knots and bows,
We dance like socks that just won't pair.
Twisted in laughter, we oppose,
The chaos found with flair.

A cat with yarn, a child's delight,
We play hide and seek with string.
Each tug a giggle, day or night,
Who knows what laughter will bring?

Our ties may tangle, that's no lie,
But who needs rules for fun?
Like spaghetti flung up high,
Let's see where the mess has run!

With every loop, we shout hooray,
Unraveled dreams in joyous flight.
So, let's get silly every day,
For bonds are made in pure delight!

Cinched Hearts

Wrapped up tight like a burrito,
We giggle as we bump and sway.
Hearts in knots, a perfect veto,
To monotony's dull ballet.

A squirrel's chase for a peanut's prize,
Our antics looped like endless tape.
With every jolt, we realize,
Life's best moments slip and scrape.

A pair of mittens, mismatched schemes,
We tug at threads with reckless glee.
In tangled joy, we live our dreams,
With knots that set our spirits free.

Each cinch a chuckle, each twist a cheer,
A bond so silly, a real delight.
In any chaos, love is near,
So let's embrace the joyful flight!

The Art of Entanglement

Twirled like a ball of silly string,
We frolic with mischief in the air.
Every twist announces spring,
As quirks and giggles we declare.

Like spaghetti thrown at the wall,
Our friendship sticks, a wobbly feast.
In every fall, we hear the call,
Of laughter rising like a beast.

With every weave, we draw a smile,
A tapestry of fun awaits.
Through tangled tales and each new mile,
We craft our bond on vivid plates.

So, let's be awkward, goofy too,
As life's a dance, a crazy show.
In every knot, we find the clue,
Together is where joy will flow!

Weaving Time Together

In looms of chaos, we embark,
With threads of laughter softly spun.
Every stitch a playful spark,
In the quilt of life, we've won!

A tug, a pull, a sudden glitch,
We trip on strings of silly fate.
Yet every laugh, just a small hitch,
In the story that we create.

Through tangled timelines, we do dance,
With every loop, our worlds align.
In every slip, we seize the chance,
To turn mishaps into a sign.

So gather 'round, let's weave our cheer,
With knots of joy that never sever.
Together here, we hold what's dear,
As life unfurls, we'll laugh forever!

The Fortitude of Binding

With shoelaces flopping everywhere,
I tripped and fell, oh, what a scare!
The dog thought it was a game to play,
As I rolled around in a tangled ballet.

My socks are mates like two peas in a pod,
They argue and bicker, oh, isn't that odd?
One claims it's the toe that needs a new friend,
While the other insists it won't ever end.

Belt loops all fighting for their true place,
Around my waist in a dizzying race!
When lunch comes calling, they're all in a twist,
And my jeans stare back like, "Why do we exist?"

But through the snags and the playful mess,
These bonds we form are simply the best!
Each knot and loop, in laughter they bind,
In the dance of life, oh, aren't we all kind?

Crossroads of Affection

Two forks collide on this dinner plate,
While spoons gossip about their fate.
Knives make comments, sharp as a jest,
"Oh, let's sit back, we're clearly the best!"

Hats stacked high like a teetering tower,
Though one's too tight, oh, what a sour!
They joke around, adding to the thrill,
"More style, less pain, could you pay the bill?"

Socks meet sandals, a match so strange,
In sunshine's glow, take on the range.
With mismatched flair, they strut their stuff,
Saying, "Fashion's not easy, but it's so much fun!"

Friendship's like tape, it stretches and bends,
It can hold us together, before it descends.
With laughter, we'll patch up all the seams,
In this silly journey of intertwining dreams!

The Harmony of Intertwining

Two strings tried to tango on the floor,
One said, "I'm done, I can't take any more!"
While rubber bands laughed, they bounced in delight,
"Oh, let's create chaos; join us tonight!"

A cat showed up, tangled in yarn,
With a pose of regality, looking so prawn!
He winked at the thread wrapped around his tail,
"We're all just a mess, but we'll prevail!"

The headphones twisted in ears like a dance,
"Let's listen to tunes, come, take a chance!
Though we tangle and knot, we'll hit every beat,
Together we'll groove, what a wonderful feat."

So let's raise a glass, to the bonds that we share,
In this circus of love, we'll always be there.
For the journey is wild, with laughter and cheer,
In the symphony of chaos, bring on the near!

Tethered by Trust

In a world where shoes come untied,
Let's hope our bond never slides.
With laughter we dance through the fray,
Double knots, please, all day!

Trust is sticky like gum on the floor,
But it bounces back—oh, we want more!
We juggle chaos like circus clowns,
With each misstep, we wear our crowns.

When that string snaps, oh what a sight,
We tie it up and say, 'That's alright!'
Through thick and thin, we surely glide,
Like socks that somehow match with pride!

So let's twirl, spin, and pirouette,
With every loop, there's no regret.
In this dance of silly embrace,
The bond we share holds its own space.

Threads of Understanding

Two threads tangled in a maze,
We laugh, we pull in messy ways.
With each tug, we learn to bend,
Twisted tales around the bend.

Life's sewing kit is quite the sight,
Funky patterns in morning light.
We stitch the quirks with happy flair,
And turn our fumbles into air.

Understanding's like a crafty needle,
Woven dreams that dance and twiddle.
Together we patch the things that fray,
Silly moments lead the way.

So let's embrace the wacky thread,
Through every laugh, no fear or dread.
In this fabric of fun and cheer,
Our crazy ties keep us near.

The Architecture of Affection

Like builders with blocks of glee,
We construct a tower, just you and me.
With laughter as our sturdy base,
We stack our memories in this space.

Each brick's a moment, a giggle shared,
A blueprint drawn, we're never scared.
As walls of love rise high and wide,
All our quirks we'll not hide!

Let's decorate with splashes of paint,
Every oddity, oh, we won't faint!
A roof of joy keeps troubles out,
Inside this house, we sing and shout.

So come on, friends, grab a tool,
In this joyful construction, we're the fool.
The labor's fun, with laughter's glue,
A masterpiece built for me and you!

Stitched with Love

Each stitch we make is a knot of fate,
Darning together, what a great state!
With fabrics of laughter, brightly sewn,
Who knew love could be such a tone?

Crooked seams and buttons askew,
We giggle and snip, then start anew.
Patchwork hearts that never tire,
With threads of joy, we caper higher.

As we quilt the memories we share,
Occasional frays, but we don't care.
In this cozy blanket of our days,
We find warmth in the silliest ways.

So let's thread this life, come what may,
With every loop, let's dance and play.
Stitched together, oh what a sight,
In this quilt of love, everything's right.

The Circle of Connection

In a world of loops and loops,
We gather like silly groups.
A twist here, a knot there,
Laughter floats in the air.

A bow on my shoe, a shoe on a cat,
Who knew ties could make us chat?
With ribbons of joy and strings of glee,
We dance like wild fools, you see!

Like spaghetti swirling in a bowl,
Each connection adds to the whole.
A jigsaw piece that fits just right,
Oh, what a silly sight at night!

So grab a friend, hold on tight,
We'll make a mess, but it feels just right.
In circles we spin, in laughter we fall,
Together we're silly, together we're all!

The Thread that Binds

A thread so fine, it weaves through jest,
From the top of my head to laces on fest.
It's not just fabric, but chuckles galore,
Pull on one end, hear the laughter roar!

We stitch our tales with patches of joy,
Knots made of giggles, oh what a ploy!
A tug on your sleeve, a wink or a grin,
In this crazy fabric, where do we begin?

With cotton candy strands and playful yarn,
We drape ourselves wide; oh dear, we can't yarn!
Swinging wildly like pendulums free,
In this silly fabric, just you wait and see!

So wrap yourself in this colorful hue,
A blend of bright laughter, just me and you.
Together we'll knot our way through the day,
In threads of camaraderie, let's forever play!

Entwined in Solace

Two worms in a garden, or so they say,
We wiggle and giggle, come join our play.
With twirls and swirls beneath the soil,
In this entangled mess, we find our toil.

Like spaghetti noodles all intertwined,
Finding true solace in every line.
A calamity of laughter in each embrace,
In the knots we make, we find our place.

So let's hold hands in this winding quest,
Finding our joy, oh what a jest!
With hugs like these, we'll never unwind,
In our puzzle of quirks, true bliss we'll find.

With every twist, may we not come apart,
In this labyrinth of laughter, you've won my heart.
Together we'll frolic, no need to be wise,
In the tangled embrace of friendship that flies!

The Clasp of Companions

Hold my hand, now take a step,
We'll clasp tight, no room for prep.
Together we wobble, together we sway,
Like a pair of clowns in our funny parade.

With a pinch and a twist, oh what a sight,
Our friendship's a clasp, oh so tight!
Mixing colors like paint in a jar,
With laughter over cups, we know who we are.

A silly handshake, a goofy grin,
We lock in our giggles and together we spin.
In this festive dance, we find our beat,
With buddies like you, life's never complete!

So here's to the bond that always stays,
In chaotic moments, in fun-filled days.
With claps and cheers, we shout out loud,
In this circus of life, we're forever proud!

The Fabric of Unity

In a world of threads so bright,
We stumble and trip, what a sight!
Unruly strings all in a bunch,
We giggle at our lunch crunch.

A patch is needed, oh dear friend,
Let's sew our laughter without end.
Stitching moments, oh what a thrill,
Our colorful chaos, a joyous drill!

We dance with fabric, twirl around,
Laughing at the knots tightly wound.
So here's to weaving tales anew,
With needle and thread, our bond is true.

Knots of Memory

Remember when we tied that shoe?
The laces danced, a lively hue.
We thought it art, a masterpiece,
But ended up in tangled fleece!

Each knot a laugh, a memory made,
Of playful pranks and how we played.
With every slip and twist we wove,
A friendship's warmth, forever strove.

Our goofy ties, like stories told,
The knots we tie, never grow old.
In every loop, a secret shared,
In tangled tales, we've always cared.

Weaving Dreams Together

Two spools of yarn, a wild affair,
We twist and twirl without a care.
Dreams once lost in the tangle here,
Are woven strong, our laughter's cheer.

With colors bright, our hopes unite,
In every twist, we take a flight.
A patchwork quilt of joy and fun,
Together we shine like the sun!

As needles click and laughter flows,
We create magic, everyone knows.
In every stitch, a vibrant thread,
A tapestry of dreams we've spread.

The Art of Linked Souls

We dance on strings, oh what a mess,
Entangled hearts, we must confess.
With every wink, our fibers sing,
Creating moments, oh what a fling!

Like puppets tied in silly glee,
We prance around, oh can't you see?
With every loop and silly fall,
Our linked souls answer the call.

So here we are, a crafty pair,
In knots of joy, beyond compare.
Let's laugh and play, embrace the fun,
With every twist, our lives are spun!

Embrace of the Elements

In the dance of summer, we're quite a pair,
With a kite that flew high and hair in the air.
The wind took our hats, what a sight to see,
Chasing those flaps, it's just you and me.

Rain came pouring, splash and giggle,
Jumping in puddles, we wiggled and wiggled.
Mud on our shoes, oh the laughter we found,
Nature's own playground, joy all around.

Snowflakes were falling, chilly delight,
We built a small fortress, a snowball fight.
Laughter erupted, as snowballs flew high,
Each throw was a memory, reaching the sky.

With every season, we share such a cheer,
Nature's embrace makes our friendship so clear.
From sun to the snow, in winds that entwine,
We joyously frolic, our spirits align.

Knots of Kindred Spirits

Twists of a friendship, a ribbon so bright,
Silly as we are, everything feels right.
You tell me my jokes, they make no sense,
Yet your laughter echoes, it's quite intense.

We tangled our yarn with no worry at all,
Creating a mess, and we had a ball.
Knots that we made while we tried to unwind,
A patchwork of giggles, hilariously blind.

Late-night whispers like a secret parade,
Sharing wild dreams that were slightly mislaid.
With ice cream in hand, we concoct the absurd,
A network of nonsense, our feelings inferred.

Our hearts are all knotted with threads spun so true,
In this crazy tapestry, it's just me and you.
Through laughter and chaos, the fabric is clear,
Kindred in madness, our joys persevere.

Interlaced Dreams

In a world full of wonders, we weave our own scheme,
With wild aspirations, we flourish and beam.
You dream up the snacks, I'll plan out the fun,
Each whim-turned-event, oh wait for the pun!

A blanket of stars, we lay on the grass,
Count every wish as the night slowly pass.
With stories all spun in a whimsical thread,
Who knew each wild tale could bring laughter instead?

Your messy concoction, a cake gone awry,
We'll scoop up the frosting and let out a cry.
With giggles a plenty, we bake up some cheer,
Each slice is a moment, cherished and dear.

Sharing our hopes like a patchwork quilt,
Interwoven together, with laughter we built.
Through dreams ever tangled, our spirits take flight,
In this joyful saga, everything feels right.

The Fabric of Friendship

Sewing up troubles with threads made of glee,
Stitch by stitch, it's just you and me.
With patches of laughter and loops of delight,
Our quirkiness weaves through the day and the night.

A fabric of colors, it ripples and sways,
In a whirlwind of humor, we brighten our days.
When life gives us shadows, we throw in a jest,
Creating a canvas that simply feels blessed.

With each tangled rumor, we laugh it away,
The fabric of trust only grows day by day.
We thread all our memories, some bold and some shy,
In the loom of our hearts, our spirits fly high.

Together we patch up the holes that arise,
With zany adventures, it's no surprise.
In the tapestry woven with each passing hour,
Our friendship's the fabric, a beautiful flower.

The Grip of Generations

Old hands teach the new tricks,
Laughter wrapped in playful mix.
Grandpa's grip, a cheeky tease,
Knotting tales with joyful ease.

Through silly pranks that bind us tight,
In family feuds, the love shines bright.
A wobbly tower of socks we make,
In each twist, a shared heartache.

Up on the porch, we string our yarn,
The ancient jokes are our sweet charm.
A tug at memories still alive,
In this mishmash, we all survive.

With dancing feet and jokes in bloom,
Generations linger in this room.
Every snicker a bond, you see,
In this knotting, we're wild and free.

The Knot of Shared Laughter

A jester's cap, the perfect bow,
With antics that steal the limelight's glow.
Strings of giggles wrap us tight,
In each chuckle, we take flight.

With wobbly chairs and funny hats,
Sharing snacks and playful chats.
In every sip of fizzy drink,
We tie the bonds with what we think.

Silly faces made in jest,
In the chaos, we find our rest.
Each pun tossed like a bouncy ball,
Behind the laughter, we stand tall.

In family trees where branches sway,
Our gags resound in a silly way.
A knot of smiles, each wrapped in cheer,
Forever cherished, year by year.

Joined at the Heart

Hearts that dance in a goofy whirl,
With a twist of fate, we laugh, we twirl.
Mismatched socks and stories grand,
In spun-up tales, we take our stand.

With every joke, our spirits lift,
In the jumble, we find our gift.
Belly laughs and accidental falls,
In this bond, the laughter calls.

Mix-up recipes, burn the bread,
Still, it's joy that fills our head.
Sharing secrets, silly and bright,
These tiny moments feel so right.

Joined by the echoes of our glee,
In this circus, we roam so free.
A bond of silliness, warm and true,
Wrapped in fun, just me and you.

Echos in the Tapestry

Threads of laughter tightly sewn,
In every stitch, a story grown.
Wacky patterns, colors bright,
We weave our joy with pure delight.

With every snip of memory made,
A tapestry of jokes displayed.
In tangled yarns and puns galore,
We find the fun behind the door.

Even when things unravel wide,
The echoes of laughter still abide.
In frayed edges, love's still taut,
In every twist, the joy is caught.

So when the fabric seems to tear,
We patch it up with love and care.
In every echo of quirky art,
We're stitched together, heart to heart.

Braid of Shared Echoes

In a world of knots and twirls,
We dance like silly squirrels.
Jokes and laughter in a spin,
With every twist, we're bound to grin.

Like shoelaces lost in a race,
Our mixed-up steps, a funny chase.
With each loop, a giggle we share,
Spinning tales in the bright air.

Bumps and tangles, oh what a tease,
We stumble forward with the best of ease.
Fuzzy threads of joyful sparks,
We tie our hearts with joyful larks.

Together, we weave a silly song,
In this web where we all belong.
A braid of echoes, laughter loud,
In the tapestry, we feel so proud.

The Loop of Life

Life's a loop that spins and spins,
With every giggle, chaos begins.
Round and round, we take the ride,
In this spiral, we laugh with pride.

Like hula hoops that wobble wide,
We find our balance, side by side.
With playful pranks and silly schemes,
We chase our dreams in teams of beams.

In each loop, new friends emerge,
We bond and twist with every surge.
Our laughter echoes, bright and spry,
A merry-go-round, oh me, oh my!

Through ups and downs, our joy remains,
In this loop, no one complains.
Together we twist, our hearts take flight,
In this dance, everything feels right.

Connective Threads

Threads of laughter fill the air,
With playful jests, we knit with care.
Each stitch a giggle, bright and loud,
In this tapestry, we feel so proud.

Oh, the fun of tangled tights,
We fall in heaps, what silly sights!
Like mismatched socks on laundry day,
We laugh it off, come what may.

Finger painting with vibrant hues,
We spin our tales like old-time news.
With every knot, new stories form,
In this patchwork, we all keep warm.

Tangled threads yet never frayed,
In this crazy mess, memories are laid.
Connected hearts that gleam and shine,
In this fabric of joy, you are mine.

Anchored Hearts

Our anchors weigh, but spirits lift,
With each oddball joke, we share our gift.
In a storm of giggles, we stay afloat,
Sailing through waves in a funny boat.

Like rubber bands that stretch and bend,
We laugh it off, we never end.
Mismatched pairs and stories grand,
Together, we are a goofy band.

With every anchor, bonds grow tight,
In the silliness, we find our light.
Nautical knits of laughter's spree,
With toes all tangled, we'd still agree.

In this sea of playful delight,
We navigate with hearts so bright.
Anchored hearts, through thick and thin,
In this sailor's tale, we always win.

Knot of Connection

In the kitchen, we spin and twirl,
The spaghetti dances, oh what a whirl!
My apron's a cape, I'm ready to cook,
But somehow I've tangled, oh what a look!

With strings of yarn, we knit with glee,
A scarf for the dog, who peeks at me.
He wears it with pride, though it's hard to wear,
He trips on the fringe, as if he's aware.

On the playground, swings soar up high,
While jump ropes make us jump 'til we cry.
I hopped over one, it wrapped 'round my knee,
Now, here comes the laughter—oh dear, woe is me!

In friendships, we tie the quirkiest bows,
With silly secrets only we knows.
Each laugh that we share, each story we weave,
Is a knot of connection, one we won't leave.

Threads of Affection

With a needle and thread, we weave our dreams,
Creating a tapestry, bursting at the seams.
A patch for the couch, but it makes me sneeze,
Did I sew it too close? Oh, how it does tease!

In the garden, we plant with a splash of cheer,
Tangled up tomatoes growing oh so near.
The vines twist and curl, in a playful spree,
I trip on a root, and yell out, "Help me!"

On video calls, we connect from afar,
But wires get crossed, like a game with a czar.
"Can you hear me now?" is the joke of the night,
As we chuckle and chat, our bonds feel just right.

With every loose thread, a smile we find,
In the messes we make, we're delightfully blind.
Each loop tells a tale, of goofs and of glee,
In the fabric of friendship, we're as close as can be.

Bound by the Breeze

A kite in the sky, dancing on air,
But hold on too tight, or it's gone without care!
The wind is a prankster, teasing our play,
It tugs at the strings, and away goes my way!

Paper airplanes soar, making wild turns,
My aim is quite off—oh, the lesson I learn.
It loops and it dives, with a swoop and a sway,
Right into a puddle! Now that's one way!

Socks in the dryer, they spin round and round,
Somehow they vanish, not a clue to be found.
They giggle and jiggle, all tangled up tight,
A sock's little party on laundry night!

Grass strands all twist in a curious knot,
As I run through the field, I trip on the spot.
Each tumble's a chuckle, each tumble's good news,
Bound by the breeze, I'll dance in my shoes!

Woven Whispers

In a web of giggles, we chat and we play,
Spinning tales round the table, night turns to day.
A whisper of secrets, so silly and light,
We've tied our own cords, what a marvelous sight!

With colorful threads, we craft our own style,
A mismatched wardrobe that brings on a smile.
The socks have their stripes, and hats have their flare,
When a laugh is the goal, do we really care?

Laughing at ourselves, we trip on our laces,
With every slip, we make funny faces.
The world is our stage, in this act we don't hide,
In woven whispers, our humor's our pride.

As we gather 'round, with snacks in a heap,
Bound by our laughter, in memories we keep.
Each quirk and each jest, an echo at play,
In a tapestry woven, we dance through the day.

Link of Legacy

In a world of knots, they twist and twirl,
Old grandma's stories make the fabric swirl.
Each loop and knot, a tale to share,
Of misadventures, laughter fills the air.

With yarn in hand, they weave their glee,
A dance of colors, wild and free.
Some strands break, but they don't mind,
For every hiccup, new fun you'll find.

Old socks and scraps form a quirky quilt,
Of mismatched fibers, with laughter built.
Each patch a memory, absurd and bright,
Together they laugh, in the soft moonlight.

So let's stitch a bond, with giddy zest,
Of silly patterns, we are truly blessed.
In every loop, a giggle grows,
Binding our hearts in woven prose.

A Dance of Threads

Two threads collide in a wobbly sway,
Fumbling their steps in a clumsy ballet.
With every twist, they pull a prank,
Leaving stitches tight, like a laughing prank.

The needle winks, a mischievous grin,
As fabrics giggle, let the chaos begin!
In this colorful jig, all rules are bent,
Where socks start dancing, and seams lament.

The buttons pop off, in a silly spree,
As ribbons skedaddle, wild and free.
A tapestry formed out of smiles so wide,
Woven together, in joy we abide.

With every twirl, a tale unfolds,
Of stitching and snitching, and treasures untold.
We'll laugh through the knots as we weave our art,
Creating a patchwork that warms every heart.

Unity in Diversity

In the fabric aisle, colors collide,
A polka dot and a stripe side by side.
Together they grumble, but laughter wins,
As denim joins floral – let the fun begin!

The patchwork quilt is quite the sight,
With funky patterns, oh what a delight!
There's a plaid that's grumpy, a paisley that sings,
A harmony crafted from odd little things.

In this crazy mix, friendships bloom,
With every stitch, they banish the gloom.
From checkered debates to solids unite,
They create a tapestry, simply out of sight!

So let's dance in colors, both vivid and bright,
Embracing our quirks, in laughter's light.
For in every twist, a story is spun,
Celebrating diversity, we're all just having fun.

Clasped Hands

Two palms come together, a silly charm,
Making shadows that dance and disarm.
With thumbs entwined, they craft a cheer,
An applause of giggles fills the air near.

Fingers interlock, in a playful embrace,
Like a knot of friendship, in a silly race.
They wave at the clouds and tickle the breeze,
Clasping in joy, as it brings them ease.

With every clasp, a giggle is shared,
A reminder of love, no strings are bared.
So join your hands in a whimsical twist,
For every connection is a moment not missed.

Together we play, in this knotty delight,
As we clasp our hands, our worries take flight.
In the dance of joy, let's spin and sway,
Creating laughter that brightens the day.

Interwoven Paths

In socks that strangely dance and prance,
A twist and shout, a merry chance.
I trip, I fall, oh what a scene,
Who knew my feet were so routine?

Laces tied in knots galore,
A game of tug, we laugh and floor.
While tangled threads begin to play,
Our giggles guide the clumsy way.

A shoelace war, a playful fight,
In chaos found, we find delight.
With every slip, a chuckle grows,
The path we take, nobody knows.

So here's to ties that pull us near,
In every knot, a tale sincere.
With every twist and loop we make,
Our friends and laughter, never break.

The Embrace of Unity

When all our hats decide to dance,
A jolly game, a funny chance.
They spin and whirl, they hug too tight,
What topsy-turvy, what a sight!

Gloves pop off like they're in a race,
Each one zips to find its place.
As sleeves entwine like a happy tune,
Our outfits clash beneath the moon.

A belt that seems to hold a grudge,
Refusing to comply or budge.
The ribbons tease, they twist and tease,
In every mess, we're sure to please.

So come together, come and see,
This tangled web of jubilee.
In every knot, a smile we share,
Together bound, without a care.

The Knot of Remembered Joys

In grandma's attic, what a find,
Old photo albums, laughs combined.
A twirl of time, we gather round,
Each snapshot tells of love unbound.

Ties of laughter wrapped so tight,
A birthday hat in silly flight.
The cake, it falls, a tasty mess,
Yet in our hearts, we feel the bless.

Remember when we dressed as clowns,
With polka dots and silly crowns?
The knots we made in childhood's name,
In every giggle, joy became.

Now every string we pull anew,
Reminds us of that vibrant hue.
In every twist, our hearts employ,
The kinks of life become our joy.

Fastened by Sentiment

In our old treehouse high and grand,
We fashioned dreams with our own hands.
A knot of twine to hold our schemes,
With every laugh, we built our dreams.

A friendship bracelet, bright and bold,
With beads of stories yet untold.
We tied a knot for each shared tale,
And every secret on the trail.

Our shoelaces tied with playful flair,
We sprinted off without a care.
In every scamper, every race,
We felt the joy light up our face.

So here's to bonds that never fray,
In silly knots, we find our way.
With silly strings that bind us tight,
Together we laugh, in pure delight.

www.ingramcontent.com/pod-product-compliance
Lightning Source LLC
Chambersburg PA
CBHW070313120526
44590CB00017B/2655